Forword

This book aims to assist any teacher who dreads writing those s‹
How frustrating is it searching for that 'appropriate' word or
students' achievements? This guide will help you to overcome those annoying mental
blocks when writing your school reports.

For organizational purposes, the words and phrases under each subject area have been
divided into two general groups, 'Experts' and 'Apprentices'. The 'Experts' are those
students who are coping very well in that subject area. The 'Apprentices' are students
who find that subject a real challenge. It's important to try and be as positive as we can
in report writing and offer some encouragement to the students even if they are really
struggling in a particular subject.

Included in this book is page full of key words and phrases to help you say the difficult
things nicely, to help write something pleasant about that difficult child.

Often teachers are required to write an overall general comment in the child's school
report. Some examples have been included to help you. These are organized under
three headings:

'**Gold**' – for the child who simply shines in all areas
'**Silver**' – for the child who copes quite satisfactorily in class.
'**Bronze**' – for the child who is struggling and finds learning a real challenge.

There's also a page titled, '100 ways to say, *very good*', as all teachers know that by the
tenth report it's a brain drain to avoid repeating ourselves! Hopefully this book will be
of some assistance, even as a springboard for your thoughts, when once again it's report
writing time.

Brett Preiss
Copyright 1996

Contents

Topic #

1. Saying the Difficult Things Nicely (school work)

Saying the difficult things nicely can often be achieved by writing something positive first, followed by a more direct comment. It's about balancing the good with the bad. Providing an alternative to negative comments leaves more room for hope for students to succeed.

About school work

- Is enthusiastic and willing, but has difficulty understanding.
- Is showing growth in his / her ability, but still needs help.
- Talks very well, but written work is a little careless.
- Conscientious and anxious to please, but has trouble keeping up with the rest of the class.
- Is beginning to enjoy working at school, but is still having trouble controlling restless energy.
- Is very co-operative in the classroom, but needs help in ….
- Is showing good growth in basic skills. However, … 's fear of rejection by classmates perhaps stops him / her from working harder in class.
- Seems to be happier and more at ease now, so it should be possible to concentrate on the basic learning skills.
- Is making rapid progress in …. but is having difficulties understanding ….
- …..'s talent for organization is not always appreciated by his / her class mates, but he/she shows initiative and dependability.
- Is becoming very dependable in the classroom, but needs to concentrate more on written work.
- Results are not a true indication of his / her ability.
- Pride and neatness in written work need to be improved.
- Tends to rush work at times.
- With increased confidence his / her work would improve a great deal.
- Needs a lot of help and encouragement.
- Spelling seems to be causing some difficulty.
- Is easily distracted and so focusing on work is a challenge.
- Finds it difficult to complete tasks on time.

2. Saying the Difficult Things Nicely (Behaviour)

About Behaviour

- Is a happy person, but rather talkative and restless in class.
- Is trying very hard to be a good student at all times.
- Is full of energy, but still has to learn there is a time for learning and a time for playing.
- When …. settles down, his/her work is excellent. I am very pleased by her/his efforts to control what is only a minor bad habit.
- ….'s natural talent for leadership means that she/he wants to manage other people, which can cause him / her unhappiness at times.
- Often seems tired and listless in school and this affects his/her work.
- …. isn't working to his / her full potential.
- Many of …..'s problems occurs in the playground and this interferes with his/her school work.
- …. finds it difficult to settle down to a quiet routine. At the moment he/she tends to seek too much help from neighbours and becomes discouraged when rebuffed.
- …. has a delightful enthusiasm for life. However, this often affects his/her ability to concentrate and focus on his/her work.
- Social relations with other children in the class are slowly improving.
- Tends to be a little lazy occasionally.
- Appears to be a little unsettled.
- Needs to be shown how to handle responsibility.
- He / she is often restless.
- Tires easily.
- Has not yet developed a good attitude to work.
- Is sometimes lacking in self-discipline and self-control.
- Easily discouraged.
- Going through a difficult period at school.
- Gradually taking part in class activities.

3. Maths / Number

Experts

- Has a positive attitude towards Maths.
- Has shown excellent understanding of mathematical concepts covered to date.
- Understands number facts (addition, subtraction etc.) very well.
- Has maintained a very high standard in Maths throughout the year.
- Has a very good memory for mathematical concepts.
- Learns new concepts quickly and easily.
- Has a solid understanding of Level … Maths concepts.
- A careful, methodical worker.
- Shows a good aptitude for number work.
- Can work on and solve problems independently.
- Has gained confidence and understanding in Maths throughout the year.
- Copes very well with extension activities.
- Number combinations are well known.
- Is good at estimating a correct answer.
- Is able to work without the help of concrete materials and a calculator.
- Has a sound knowledge of mathematical principles.
- Understands most processes and rules.

Apprentices

- With regular revision …..'s Math's concepts would be well consolidated.
- Copes better with practical Math's activities rather than theory.
- ….. needs extra support with Maths.
- Can often be careless with number work.
- ….. doesn't find number work easy but he/she is slowly becoming more confident.
- Has poor knowledge of processes and rules.
- Has a lot of difficulty with problem work.
- Too dependent on concrete materials.
- Unable to reason clearly when solving math problems.
- …. needs to work a lot harder in this area to become confident with Maths.

4. Reading

Experts

- Reads accurately and with expression.
- Comprehension skills are strong.
- A very expressive reader.
- An independent reader.
- Makes use of the library books and does extra reading outside school.
- Attacks new and difficult words with confidence.
- Reads enthusiastically.
- Has a good knowledge of vocabulary.
- Understands well what he/she reads.
- Selects and reads good literature.
- Reads fluently / fervently / avidly.
- Has a great enthusiasm for reading.
- Reads a wide range of genres.
- Has great word-recognition skills.
- Competent word attack skills.
- Can recall the main ideas of a story well and in sequence.
- Has good prediction skills.
- Can identify the main events in a story well.
- Can identify the author's message from a story.
- Can retell a story in own words.

Apprentices

- Reads slowly, but accurately.
- Is making steady progress with reading.
- Very selective with what he/she wants to read.
- Needs a lot of individual support and guidance with reading.
- Doesn't show a lot of interest in books and reading.
- Finds reading a real challenge.
- Confident in basic reading skills.
- Prefers to have stories read to him/her.
- Extra reading at home would prove beneficial.
- Confidence and fluency will improve with shared-reading strategies.

5. Spelling

Experts

- A competent speller.
- Has a high spelling ability.
- An excellent speller who learns new words easily.
- Can spell new words accurately.
- Has a good visual memory for spelling.
- Has developed good strategies for remembering new/difficult words.
- Makes good use of phonetic sounds.
- Employs common spelling rules.
- Is good at word building and grouping activities.
- Knowledge of word families is good.
- Has the ability to discern word structure.
- Does very well with dictations.
- Has sound spelling sense.
- Consistently obtains high scores in spelling tests.
- Vocabulary and spelling skills have been of a high standard throughout the year.
- Often displays accurate spelling in general work.
- Reading ability enhances spelling skills.
- Has a good knowledge of spelling rules.

Apprentices

- Reads slowly, but accurately.
- Needs to develop his/her visual memory for spelling.
- A greater effort with spelling practice at school and home is required.
- Relies too much on phonics when spelling.
- Carelessness in pronunciation causes problems with spelling correctly.
- Does not apply simple spelling rules.
- Finds spelling a real challenge.
- Needs to have basic spelling lists constantly revised.
- Requires a lot of support with spelling strategies.
- Spelling has improved slowly, but surely.

6. Writing

Experts

- Can use imagination well in writing.
- Uses punctuation well.
- Can express thoughts clearly in writing.
- Written work is creative and original.
- Has an extensive vocabulary and uses it well.
- Writes independently.
- Always confident in writing.
- A fluent writer.
- Uses language effectively.
- Can write in a variety of genres.
- Writing shows strong literacy skills.
- Can organize thoughts and ideas well.
- Can write for different audiences.
- Always self-edits work.
- Has a strong understanding of the conventions of writing.
- Writes organized, fluent and accurate non-fiction.
- Writes cohesive and effective fiction.
- Uses a lot of literary devices in writing e.g. imagery, metaphors.
- Has developed his/her own personal style of writing.

Apprentices

- Can write simple, meaningful sentences.
- Is beginning to express his/her thoughts in writing.
- Writing often lacks original ideas.
- Is beginning to use imagination in stories.
- Work often contains too many grammatical errors.
- Needs to develop knowledge of punctuation.
- Takes risks with writing but needs a lot of support.
- Needs guidance to add details to writing.
- Benefits from dictating a story and having it written out to copy.
- Prefers to tell stories than to write.

7. Handwriting

Experts

- Fluent writer.
- Has correct posture.
- Correct pencil hold at all times.
- Shape and slope of letters are always neat, accurate and consistent.
- Always neat and legible.
- Handwriting is a lovely style and easy to read.
- Writes with fluency, rhythm and reasonable speed.
- Writing is consistently neat and well presented in all books.
- Controls and uses pencils correctly.
- Shows pride in all written work.
- Can write quickly and neatly.
- Shows good letter and number formation.
- Maintains a high standard with his/her handwriting.
- Very good hand/eye coordination.
- Shows tidiness in all written work.
- Has a good knowledge of basic letterforms.
- Shows skills in slope, size, shape and spacing.
- Writes legibly.

Apprentices

- Is slowly developing correct letter formation.
- Finds handwriting difficult.
- Sometimes rushes work, which makes it difficult to read.
- Poor shape and formation of letters.
- More practice and care is needed with handwriting.
- Writes slowly and has difficulty completing tasks on time.
- Incorrect pencil grip makes it difficult for him/her to form letters properly.
- Needs to develop skills with size and formation of letters.
- Needs to work on presentation and neatness.
- Letter formations need to be more consistent in size and shape.
- Is beginning to try different forms of writing from printing to cursive.
- Intermixes upper and power case letters.
- Needs to use spaces between words more consistently.

8. Listening

Experts

- Can listen and follow with understanding and interest.
- Listens well.
- Can follow simple directions.
- Listens attentively.
- Can listen with empathy.
- Listens without interrupting others.
- Is a sensitive listener.
- Listens purposefully.
- Listens with an open mind.
- Listens reflectively.
- Listens with comprehension.
- Listens carefully.
- Can listen critically and distinguish fact from opinion.
- Listens creatively.
- Listens appreciatively.
- Listens closely.
- Shows good auditory discrimination.
- Listens analytically.
- Recalls accurately in sequence what he/she had heard.

Apprentices

- Listens passively.
- Is learning how to develop listening skills.
- Listens intermittently.
- Relies on repeated instructions.
- Listens narrowly.
- Needs to pay more attention.
- Has difficulty in focusing.
- Needs to place more emphasis on listening.
- Is developing listening skills.
- A selective listener.
- A good listener on occasion.
- Needs to listen carefully to gain understanding of the listening process.

9. Talking

Experts

- Is fluent and confident in speaking.
- Reveals originality in oral expression.
- Always has valuable thoughts and ideas to share with the class.
- He/she is a keen participant in all lessons.
- Confident when expressing his/her own ideas and opinions and generally supports answers well.
- Is uninhibited in expression of opinion.
- Has ability to articulate ideas.
- Converses freely.
- Confident, friendly attitude in conversation.
- Speaks clearly about experiences.
- Has the ability to hold an audience.
- Speaks clearly and with good expression.
- Talks correctly and distinctly.
- Has a wide vocabulary.
- Participates freely in oral discussion.
- Speaks audibly.
- Purposeful speaker.
- Communicates easily.
- Has the ability to sustain an argument.
- Confident when speaking aloud.

Apprentices

- Sometimes reluctant to converse.
- Lacking in confidence.
- Timid speaker.
- Takes little part in oral work.
- Somewhat shy and lacking in confidence.
- Has difficulty with clear oral expression.
- Speaks too softly.
- Needs to build on his/her self confidence.
- Has difficulty making a personal response to discussion.
- Needs encouragement to participate in oral activities.
- Needs to become more aware of appropriate language in different situations.
- Shows development in the effective use of spoke language.

10. Science and Technology

Experts

- Shows interest and curiosity.
- Is developing a sound knowledge of the world around him/her.
- Has an avid interest in science.
- Is involved with many explanatory type activities.
- Asks many questions of a provocative nature.
- Has an interest in cause–effect relations.
- Contributes well to lessons.
- Lesson participation is good and work is always well completed.
- Shows strong interest in all topics covered.
- Has an inquiring mind.
- Is very interested in science.
- Is developing research skills.
- Shows interest in developing computer skills.
- Has an understanding of computer use.
- Can work independently with computers.
- Particularly enjoys the 'hands-on' activities.
- Loves to manipulate materials.
- Can evaluate and use the products of technology well.
- Makes informed judgements concerning natural and man-made environments.
- Enjoys exploring and discovering new things.
- Is capable of carrying out an investigation.
- Can select and use a range of technologies.

Apprentices

- Is slowly developing an interest in Science and Technology.
- Prefers 'hands-on' activity to knowledge and theory.
- Could show more interest, particularly in discussion.
- Not very interested in science.
- Reluctant to try and solve problems.
- Shows little interest in learning about the world around him/her.
- Prefers to work in a group rather than independently on tasks.
- Has difficulty drawing conclusions from science activities.
- Needs more confidence in using technology and equipment.
- Prefers to work alone rather than collaboratively in group tasks.
- Highly dependent on team members when participating in group tasks.
- Needs additional supervision to remain on task.

11. Social Studies
(Human Society & its Environment)

Experts

- Displays a great curiosity about objects, situations and events.
- Immensely interested in the world around him.
- An inquiring mind is developing.
- Has sound general knowledge of this area.
- Is good at mapping.
- Undertakes independent reading and research.
- Project work has been well researched and well presented.
- Understands basic concepts.
- Competent in making inferences.
- Shows ability to interpret information.
- Is able to research well and organize data.
- Is able to apply principles learned.
- Han an inquisitive nature.
- Can seek, acquire and record information well.
- Reads and interprets diagrams, maps and graphs well.
- Appreciates and enjoys learning about new cultures.
- Shows concern for the environment.
- Takes intelligent interest in local and world events.

Apprentices

- Could show more interest, particularly in discussion.
- General knowledge is limited.
- Could take more care with book work.
- Suggest wider reading in this subject.
- Needs to be shown various modes of presenting project work.
- Not very interested in Social Studies.
- Usually completes set tasks.
- Inconsistent with homework and project work.
- Needs to further develop understanding of cultural differences.
- Sometimes has difficulty in interpreting maps and diagrams.
- Prefers to work alone rather than collaboratively in group tasks.
- Needs further experiences to make connection between the issues studied and his/her own environment.

12. Art / Craft

Experts

- Draws a variety of subjects.
- Puts depth into work, plans and uses good proportion.
- Takes Art/Craft work seriously, finding much satisfaction in it.
- Often shows originality in his/her work.
- Is willing to try new material and experiences.
- Fills extra time with artistic activities.
- Uses Art to express his/her own experiences and feelings.
- Is often interested in and appreciates other people's artwork.
- Can appreciate, criticize, and learn from other's work.
- Likes to model with clay, plasticine etc.
- Shows a good feeling for colour.
- Blends colours artistically.
- Exhibits confidence in composition.
- Has ability for drawing and sketching.
- Has a flair for art/craft work.
- Draws/paints creatively.
- Work is always creative and neat.
- Has developed good techniques with different media.
- Has a good understanding of the principles of element and design.
- Shows pride in the finished product.

Apprentices

- Shows little interest in this area.
- Taking part in art/craft activities requires more effort.
- Dislikes the messy side of art/craft.
- Finds it difficult to express him/her self through the Visual Arts.
- Could show greater appreciation in other people's artwork.
- Lacks confidence and imagination in this area.
- Finds creative expression tedious / difficult.
- Needs extra support and tuition in this area.
- Would benefit from a more positive attitude towards art/craft.
- Needs to be prepared to try all areas of art/craft.
- Could be more considerate when using or packing away art/craft materials.
- Needs to co-operate and work as a team during group tasks.

13. Music

Experts

- Has a good sense of rhythm.
- Has excellent discrimination of sounds.
- Understands musical symbols and notation.
- Shows enjoyment of musical activities.
- Enjoys performing.
- Has a good memory of songs / tunes.
- Plays one or more musical instruments well and / or sings well.
- Is very interested in musical activities.
- Can create original tunes.
- Enjoys dancing and moving to music.
- Participates in all musical activities.
- Enjoys performing in a choir.
- Is developing a good knowledge of musical vocabulary.
- Can communicate ideas and feelings well through music.
- Developing good techniques in all areas of Music.
- A musical production manager in the making!

Apprentices

- Needs to develop a more positive attitude towards music.
- Dislikes performing and creating music.
- Finds it difficult to listen to and appreciate music.
- It takes a lot of effort to encourage …. to sing, play and move.
- …. finds little satisfaction in music.
- Recognition of and response to sound are poor.
- Finds it difficult to understand the concepts of music.
- Has very little interest in singing or choir work.
- Music is not his/her favourite subject.
- Reluctant to experience a variety of musical styles.
- Shows little enthusiasm for learning to play an instrument.
- More self-discipline is required in music lessons.
- Needs to be more attentive when responding to instructions in music lessons.
- Displays some interest in this area; extra tuition would see positive results.

14. Drama

Experts

- Readily shifts into the role of another character, animal or subject.
- Shows a lot of interest in drama activities.
- Can use his/her voice well to reflect various roles.
- Communicates feelings by means of facial expressions and experiences.
- Gets a good deal of satisfaction and happiness from play-acting or dramatizing.
- Enjoys acting.
- Has a flair for Drama.
- Enjoys drama activities.
- Is good at organizing texts, props, costumes etc.
- Works expertly in mime activities.
- Is very good at characterization and expressing him/her self.
- Confident when performing.
- Loves to be involved in all Drama activities.
- Shows great potential in acting and performance.
- Enjoys working and performing with others.
- Remembers parts for plays very well.

Apprentices

- Shows very little interest in Drama activities.
- Lacks confidence in expressing him/her self.
- Dislikes Drama as a means of communication.
- Dislikes performing and role creating.
- It takes a lot of effort to encourage …. to participate in activities.
- Reluctant to take a risk and 'have a go'.
- Needs a lot of encouragement and individual attention before trying an activity.
- Enjoys plays and character work but doesn't enjoy movement activities.
- Has difficulty in responding to Drama activities.
- Working and performing with others are a challenge.
- Is intimidated by large scale performances.
- Has difficulty participating in improvisation activities in Drama.
- Is slowly developing the skills for voice projection and expression in presentations.

15. Sport / Physical Education

Experts

- Is acquiring good balance and co-ordination.
- Shows aptitude in this area.
- Is acquiring basic skills of kicking, catching, throwing, hopping, skipping etc.
- Enjoys sport and playing a variety of games.
- Is very athletic.
- Enjoys team sports.
- Prominent in all school sports.
- Likes to play.
- Has body build conducive to physical activities.
- Is well coordinated.
- Spends extra time after school in physically oriented activities.
- Is always active and energetic.
- Excellent gross motor skills.
- Is confident in all physically oriented activities.
- Participates well in group activities.
- Exhibits skill in Physical Education.
- Participates willingly in all sports and physical education activities.
- Strong competitive spirit with all sports.
- Displays sportsmanship.
- Uses sense in playground behavior.
- Is developing co-ordination / strength / flexibility / body awareness.

Apprentices

- Is not interested in physical activities.
- Needs to exert more effort.
- Has poor gross motor skills and co-ordination.
- Dislikes team sports.
- Prefers individual fitness activities to team sports.
- Shows a lack of enthusiasm for sport.
- Needs to develop more confidence in sport and physical education.
- Not inclined to have a competitive attitude with sports.
- Improvement needed in sportsmanship.
- Needs to develop body awareness and co-ordination.
- Not keen to participate in a wide variety of sports
- Has a low level of fitness
- .... is not very fit, physically.

16. Words of Gold, Silver and Bronze

Gold	Silver	Bronze
Industrious	Good	Fair
Energetic	Perservering	Timid
Conscientious	Steady	Stubborn
Reliable	Appreciative	Immature
Excellent	Encouraged	Restless
Alert	Balanced	Boisterous
Co-operative	Tolerant	Unresponsive
Enthusiastic	Composed	Aggressive
Diligent	Considerate	Placid
Delightful	Good tempered	Hostile
Mature	Happy	Show-off
Responsible	Modest	Awkward
Achiever	Neat	Devious
Independent	Orderly	Fidgety
Self-controlled	Patient	Hot tempered
Advanced	Sensitive	Impatient
Successful	Stable	Impulsive
Articulate	Tidy	Irresponsible
Knowledge	Improving	Unambitious
Dynamic	Progressing	Serious
Vivacious	Reasonable	Disagreeable
Zealous	Aware	Slow
Dedicated	Co-operative	Shy
Competent	Sensible	Inattentive
Admirable	Adequate	Confused
Meritorious	Average	Inconsistent
Ambitious	Capable	Passable
Courteous	Dependable	Disobedient
Imaginative	Interested	Impolite
Talented	Well-adjusted	Withdrawn

17. Social / Emotional Development

Gold

- Respects the property of others as well as his/her own.
- Plays fairly and sensibly
- A very caring, helpful student, always assisting others.
- Is very secure emotionally.
- Has ability to get along with a wide variety of individuals.
- Is looked to by others when decisions must be made or actions taken.
- Has mature social skills.
- Observes school and class rules
- Has keen sense of humour.
- Sees the funny side of any situation.
- Practices self-discipline.
- Manners, speech and deportment are exemplary.

Silver

- Is gaining confidence in him/her self
- Relates well to peers.
- Has diverse interests.
- Can help organize others.
- Willingly supports others when needed.
- Is friendly and outgoing.
- Is independent.
- Observes School and Class rules.
- Is courteous and well mannered.
- Has a good sense of humour.
- Takes good care of school equipment.
- Rarely needs discipline.

Bronze

- Not always generous or charitable to others.
- Resents advice and assistance on occasions.
- Somewhat lacking in self-confidence.
- Sometimes forgetful in manners and speech.
- Inclined to remain aloof from others.
- Can have a negative influence on others.
- Can be talkative at times.
- Demands excessive attention.
- Lacks confidence.
- Has much energy which needs rechanneling at times.
- Tends to dominate peers or situations.

18. Work Habits

Gold

- Conduct and attitude to work are excellent.
- Works well independently.
- Can concentrate well.
- Is co-operative and enthusiastic.
- Creative in thoughts and new ideas.
- Always maintains a high standard of bookwork.
- Able to work without supervision.
- Does his/her best at all times.
- Confident in his/her own ability.
- Is innovative.
- Very alert, often gives rapid answers.

Silver

- Learns quickly and efficiently.
- Joins in activities.
- Shows pride in bookwork.
- Uses spare time sensibly.
- Has a long attention span.
- Is keen to extend knowledge.
- Shows ambition and a desire to do well.
- Working to capacity.
- Making good progress.
- Shows perseverance and initiative.

Bronze

- Trying to improve.
- Needs close guidance with most work.
- Lacks consistent effort.
- Could take more care with bookwork.
- Sometimes neglectful with homework.
- Not working to capacity.
- Needs more encouragement.
- Is beginning to settle down in class.
- Needs more help at home.
- Somewhat lacking in drive and interest.
- Needs help to improve standard of work.

19. Pro Formas of General Comments
To help conclude your report.

Student names and subjects have been **italicized** in the following comments. Simply change the words to suit your purpose!

Gold

1. *Peter* is a conscientious student who can organize his time well and use it effectively. He has made very good progress this year. *Peter* works independently, diligently, and has improved immensely with his decision making. He is keen to learn and enjoys school. I feel *Peter* will cope well with the challenges and stimulation of the next grade.

2. *Anita* has been an enthusiastic and conscientious student. Academically, she has been a hard-working student with a love for *Literature* and *learning*. *Anita*'s school work has been of a very good standard all year. She possesses a mature disposition with a co-operative and good humoured approach to all tasks. *Anita* is a responsible and dependable student. It has been an absolute pleasure to work with *Anita* throughout this year and I am confident she will continue to do well next year. I wish her all the best.

3. *Helen* is and always has been, an independent and achievement-orientated student. Academically, she is an excellent student with a vigilant and enquiring approach to learning. Her school work has been of a very high standard reflecting a rich and supportive home environment. *Helen* possesses a delightful, methodical disposition with a co-operative approach to all tasks. She has a well-adjusted commonsense approach towards her own abilities. *Helen* has achieved high levels of competence in *English* and *Maths* and possesses excellent *communication skills*. She has held the respect of all staff members at school. *Helen* is a student of exceptional qualities and strongly emerging creative talents. I am confident that she will continue to be a successful student. I predict that many teachers will in the years ahead, enjoy making the claim, "I taught her!"

Pro Formas of General Comments *(continued)*

Silver

1. ***Troy*** loves working with other children in group situations. Attendance at the ***Art*** and ***Drama*** camp this year has inspired his creativity and spontaneity. This has become evident in all aspects of his work. ***Troy*** has a positive, self-confident approach to most tasks. His sense of humour is an asset to his well-developed social skills.

2. Despite a slow start, ***Tina*** has progressed well this year. She is a bright girl, and when she applies herself she is capable of producing a very good standard of work. ***Tina*** has worked steadily at improving her *reading* this year, and has developed a good understanding of ***mathematical concepts***. Her ***writing*** has also improved steadily and displays a very good imagination. ***Tina***'s creativity also shines through in her ***visual arts*** work, for which she shows great enthusiasm and achieves a high level of competence. ***Tina*** works well on her own, and is a lively participant in classroom discussions.

3. ***Rory***'s main area of interest is ***reading***, which he does independently. ***Maths*** is showing some improvement. ***Rory*** has particularly enjoyed ***fractions*** and ***geometry,*** and is starting to work independently. He has a good imagination. However, with motivation, ***Rory*** could write very interesting stories. ***Rory*** enjoys discussions during most subjects. His opinions are often well thought out and well presented. ***Rory*** has produced some creative, talented ***visual art*** work and enjoys experimenting with ***colours*** and ***prints***. Regarding ***spelling***, he has to apply himself, and build up his confidence to enable more of his imagination to flow into his writing. ***Rory's handwriting*** is particularly neat and he can be a real perfectionist in this area. Keep up the good effort!

Pro Formas of General Comments *(continued)*

Bronze

1. *Christie* has progressed steadily throughout the year, accelerating most when individual assistance has been given and when she is dealing with topics of interest to her. She is a learner who requires variety and stimulation, and activities with instructions that are concise, easy to follow and well structured. She appears to be listening well as she has become more confident and independent in her participation in lessons and in group work. The most notable change in *Christie* this year has been the improvement in her personal confidence. She will now attempt new work without anxiety. I have enjoyed working with *Christie* and getting to know her. She has a polite, co-operative nature and a delightful sense of humour. I am confident she will continue to improve.

2. *Clint* has worked steadily throughout the year showing some progress in areas such as *Reading, Handwriting* and *Maths*. The support *Clint* has been given at school and at home needs to be continued further develop his confidence in learning and doing his schoolwork. Wit continued encouragement *Clint* will see some improvement in his *learning skills*. Progress comes with perseverance.

3. *Chloe* needs more encouragement and discipline in order to develop her confidence and to work to her true ability. I feel that *Chloe* needs constant revision and continued one-to-one instruction to help her overcome the challenges and the frustrations found in her work. I am sure that she will make progress next year with continued support.

100 Ways to Say, "Very Good"

1. You're on the right track.	51. You've got it made.
2. You are doing a good job.	52. This is so good.
3. You have done so much work.	53. Nothing can stop you now.
4. Well done.	54. This is it!
5. You have figured it out!	55. You are very good at this.
6. That's right!	56. You are learning fast.
7. Now you've got the hang of it.	57. I'm very proud of you.
8. That's the way.	58. You certainly did well.
9. Now you have it.	59. You just about go it.
10. Brilliant.	60. What a masterpiece.
11. Nice going.	61. I'm so happy to see you working like this.
12. That's great.	62. That's the right way to do it.
13. You did it that time.	63. You are really learning a lot.
14. Fantastic!	64. This better than ever.
15. This is coming along nicely.	65. This is quite an improvement.
16. Good work.	66. This kind of work makes me very happy.
17. That's better.	67. You've got it now.
18. Excellent.	68. Well done .....
19. Terrific.	69. Fine work.
20. This is really good work.	70. That's a lot of creative thinking.
21. Good job	71. Not half bad!
22. You outdid yourself this time.	72. That's incredible.
23. This is the best you have ever done.	73. You have a great memory.
24. Keep up the good work.	74. This shows you listened well.
25. Great going.	75. I think you have go it now.
26. Wow!	76. Well, look at you go!
27. Good for you.	77. You are showing great understanding.
28. This is really wonderful.	78. Tremendous
29. Marvellous.	79. Outstanding
30. Keep up the pleasing work.	80. Couldn't have done better myself.
31. Your work is thorough and detailed.	81. Great perseverance.
32. Exactly right!	82. Congratulations.
33. Super!	83. Now that's what I call a fine job.
34. Bravo!	84. You did that very well.
35. I'm impressed.	85. That's the best!
36. That's much better.	86. Everything is just right.
37. You make it look so easy.	87. This is first class work.
38. You are doing much better.	88. I really like this.
39. This is really beautiful work.	89. Sensational!
40. Superb.	90. Well completed.
41. Wonderful.	91. This is the best ever.
42. You are getting better every day.	92. What a good memory.
43. You are making great progress.	93. It's such a pleasure to work with you.

44. I knew you could do it.	94. You haven't missed a thing.
45. Keep working on it, you are doing well.	95. Your work is exemplary.
46. You are doing beautifully.	96. You are really clever.
47. Nicely done.	97. I knew you could do it.
48. You are really working hard.	98. I am so proud of you.
49. This is the way to do it. Excellent.	99. You figured this out fast.
50. Keep on trying.	100. Your work is of high quality.

Printed in Great Britain
by Amazon